WORKBOOK FOR

CODEPENDENT NO MORE

(A Guide to Melody Beattie's Book)

Your Powerful Guide to Stop Controlling Others and Start Caring for Yourself

<u>ABOUT MELODY BEATTIE</u>

Beattie is among the most popular writers in the genre of self-help in the United States. Following a spiritual epiphany, she left her life as an addict to become a self-help book.

In the fields of addiction and rehabilitation, she is a household name. In 1986, Beattie's 'Codependent No More' became a worldwide bestseller and is widely credited with popularizing the term "codependency." Over the course of her 24-year writing career (as of June 2022), she has published roughly 18 books in 20 different languages. Beattie has also contributed numerous essays to various periodicals.

On July 2, 1948, Melody Beattie entered this world in Saint Paul, Minnesota. It is unknown who or what her parents are.

After her father left, her mother was left to raise her and her siblings. Beattie's alcoholism began at the tender age of twelve. After finishing college, she went to work as a secretary in the advertising industry. At 18, she started abusing drugs and alcohol, which only made her alcoholism worse.

Melody Beattie had two weddings. In 1970, she wed Steven Thurik for the first time. With her first spouse, she had a son they called John Steven Thurik. Because of her drinking problem, they split up in 1973. Melody's addiction caused her to relinquish custody of their son to her husband. After some time, she checked into a rehab facility.

Beattie eventually overcame her substance abuse problem and married David Anthony Beattie. David Beattie worked as a therapist for alcoholics. With David, she had twins.

Nichole Marie and Shane Anthony Beattie are their children's names. In 1986, Melody and David Anthony Beattie got a divorce. In 1991, her son Shane was killed in a skiing accident.

Beyond Codependency, Codependent No More, The Language of Letting Go, and Make Miracles in Forty Days: Turning What You Have into What You Want are some of Beattie's most well-known works. She had a lot of books translated into different languages.

Melody's drug abuse persisted until she experienced a profound realization.

In 1986, her book "Codependent No More" came out. Nearly eight million copies were sold, and the book is credited with popularizing the concept of codependency. The organization Hazelden published the book.

Beattie, Janet G. Woititz, and Robin Norwood wrote a book called "Diagnosing and Treating Co-Dependence," which Beattie summarized and helped the listener understand.

A precursor to "The Big Book," Beattie's early writings were influential among members of Co-Dependents Anonymous. Conference approval has been given to the 12-step program known as CoDA. The tests at CoDA conferences revolve around her writings.

THIS ONE WEEK OUTLINE WAS DEVELOPED TO HELP YOU.

➢ The foremost thing
  is to find a
  person you can rely on to
   help you achieve your
  goals if you want to be
  successful.

➢ Be careful not
  to make any mistakes
  when filling out the vital
  forms displayed below.

➢ Consider each day's tip,
  task and prescription
  carefully.

THINK ABOUT THEM MEDITATIVELY.

> Everything you learned in the note should be written and meditated upon.

Also, jot down your thoughts and feelings, as well as the obstacles you've come to terms with.

READ AND LISTEN TO
EVERYTHING
THAT IS BEING SAID
AND RECOMMENDED.

Without a doubt, adhere to
them.

**IT WAS MADE TO BE
POSSIBLE.**

Never doubt the fact that
you
can do it, and never give up
hope.

**YOU'RE ALL SET TO STEP
ON TO THE NEXT LEVEL!**

Ensure that you fill out the
Form below in its entirety.

DATE IT ALL BEGINS

_____

_____

DATE OF FINAL
CONCLUSION (Usually 7 D
ays from the starting Date)

_____

Fill in the blanks with your
name and email address:

_____

_____

FILL OUT YOUR AGE

_____

_____

**It's not as difficult as you might
think, but don't take it for
granted and keep going.**

Recommendations and
Tasks for the Day Don't End
That Day; Carry On and
Make Habits of Them.

DAY 1

INSIGHT

Realize that you cannot be truly happy without money but you'd be happier than ever with money and without a job. As an adult, am sure nobody would be truly interested in catering for all your expenses.

WHAT YOU SHOULD IMBIBE TODAY

You need to put in work once and for all to be getting some cash at least. Find a business model (passive income) that has the ability of generating sufficient revenue from nothing. I suggest listing a digital product to the market or an online service managed by others.

<u>DON'T FORGET…</u>

True happiness and freedom cannot
be attained without money, that'd be
self-deceit.

MEDITATE

_____

_____

_____

_____

_____

_____

_____

_____

_____

_____

_____

_____

_____

_____

_____

_____

_____

_____

_____

_____

_____

_____

_____

_____

_____

_____

_____

_____

_____

**The first step to this is getting
'automatic' money.**

DAY 2

INSIGHT

Liberty and happiness does not come from idleness. Being busy during the day with hobbies, adventures, things and people you love is the way to this.

WHAT YOU SHOULD IMBIBE TODAY...

Discover those things you love doing that are good for you. Have a weekly plan of your hobbies, travels, adventures and hanging out with friends.

DON'T FORGET...

No idle and sane person can truly
claim to be happy. We are humans,
we were made to explore.

MEDITATE

_____

_____

_____

_____

_____

_____

_____

_____

_____

_____

_____

_____

_____

_____

_____

_____

_____

_____

_____

_____

_____

_____

_____

_____

_____

_____

**The idle mind is indeed
devil's workshop.**

DAY 3

INSIGHT

Realize today that health is wealth, health is everything. A sick person can neither have happiness nor liberty.

WHAT YOU SHOULD IMBIBE TODAY

End unhealthy lifestyle and practices. Stop drugs, smoking, alcohol and unhealthy diet. Stop all forms of unhealthy and unfavorable behaviors.

DON'T FORGET...

Don't ever jeopardize or compromise health for fun, you'd regret it terribly.

MEDITATE…

_____

_____

_____

_____

_____

_____

_____

_____

_____

_____

_____

_____

_____

_____

_____

_____

_____
_____
_____
_____
_____
_____
_____
_____
_____
_____

**Good health is your biggest
asset.**
_____

DAY 4

INSIGHT

Exercises and good night rest have been proven to add more light to your entire life. This lifestyle strengthens your cells and influences your happiness and freedom,

WHAT YOU SHOULD IMBIBE TODAY

Go to bed early, rise early and exercise your body every morning. This lifestyle alone would add to your length of days and strength at old age.

<u>DON'T FORGET...</u>

Even if you don't have huge resources for a good life, practicing good night rest and morning exercises would enable you stay good.

MEDITATE

_____

_____

_____

_____

_____

_____

_____

_____

_____

_____

_____

_____

_____

_____

_____

_____

_____

_____

_____

_____

_____

_____

_____

_____

_____

_____

_____

**Exercising and having a good
night rest isn't costly.**

DAY 5

INSIGHT

Overburdening yourself with life troubles (Both yours and those of others) is one of the surest ways of living a miserable life..

WHAT YOU SHOULD IMBIBE TODAY...

Do the things you can do and leave the rest. You don't deserve carry all burdens, they'd kill you sooner.

DON'T FORGET

If you die today, the world will still
forget you and move regardless of
how important you might think you
are. Those problems would still be
solved one way or the other.

MEDITATE

_____

_____

_____

_____

_____

_____

_____

_____

_____

_____

_____

_____

_____

_____

_____

_____

_____

_____

_____

_____

_____

_____

_____

_____

_____

Stop giving a f*ck.

DAY 6

INSIGHT

Your diet lifestyle has a very powerful role to play in your life and personal well-being. You should never forget this fact.

WHAT YOU SHOULD IMBIBE TODAY

End all forms of unhealthy diet today. Don't eat out of impulse. Get a healthy food plan and stick to eat.

DON'T FORGET

Bad feeding has negative impact on your health and well-being. Avoid bad food at all cost.

MEDITATE

_____

_____

_____

_____

_____

_____

_____

_____

_____

_____

_____

_____

_____

_____

_____

_____

_____

_____

_____

_____

_____

_____

_____

_____

_____

_____

**Rather go hungry than eat
unhealthy dishes.**

DAY 7

INSIGHT

The place where you stay has been proven to have great impact on your mood, health and general well-being. It is advisable to try as much as possible to live in comfortable, less toxic and neat places.

WHAT YOU SHOULD IMBIBE TODAY

If the place you live destroys your self-worth, emotions, and mood or saps your energy, leave there immediately. If it isn't neat and organized, put in the work now.

DON'T FORGET

Be neat at all times because
cleanliness is next to Godliness!!!

MEDITATE

_____

_____

_____

_____

_____

_____

_____

_____

_____

_____

_____

_____

_____

_____

_____

_____

_____

_____

_____

_____

_____

_____

_____

_____

_____

_____

_____

_____

The place you live tells a lot about you!

YOU'VE FINISHED WITHTHIS ONE WEEK GUIDE. KEEP UP WITH IT.

POSITIVE RESULT COMES WITH IT.

Show Love to people by giving them copies of this.

_____

_____

_____

_____

_____

_____

_____

_____

_____

_____

_____

_____

_____

_____

_____

_____

BYE!

Each time you're deviating, return to this!

Made in the USA
Las Vegas, NV
22 November 2024

12404699R00026